1

EASY DOES IT. THIS IS TELEPORTING A HUMAN BEING, NOT USING THE BLENDER FOR ONE OF YOUR PROTEIN SHAKES.

BLENDER, TELEPORTER, SAME THING—ALL I HAVE TO DO IS PUSH A BUTTON!

NO, WAIT!

PUMP! LOOK WHAT YOU DID! YOU PRESSED IT TOO SOON!

OOPS?

WHERE AM I? WHO ARE YOU GUYS?

DID I JUST LAND ON SOMEONE?

GRASH!!!

IT'S OKAY, I'M BUILT WITH LOTS OF EXTRA CUSHIONING!

IN THE BLOODSTREAM.

WHOA!

BLOOD TRAVELS THROUGH YOUR BODY IN *PIPES* CALLED *BLOOD VESSELS.*

THEY ARE ALL AROUND YOUR BODY AND DIVIDE LIKE BRANCHES ON A TREE.

COOL! LOOK AT THOSE PIPES!

THE BRANCHES GET SMALLER AND SMALLER AS THEY SPREAD THROUGHOUT YOUR *WHOLE BODY,* EVEN TO THE TIPS OF YOUR FINGERS AND TOES!

BUT YOU DON'T HAVE FINGERS OR TOES.

UH, GUYS! WE'VE GOT A BREACH IN THE BLOOD VESSEL!

WE HAVE A *WHAT?*

THERE'S A BREAK IN THE PIPE.

6

WHAT'S HAPPENING?

IT SEEMS WE ARE BEING PULLED OUT WITH THE REST OF THE BLOOD CELLS. THIS COULD BE PROBLEMATIC.

EXPLAIN PROBLEMATIC!

FINALLY, HAVING FOUR LUNCHES A DAY IS PAYING OFF!

WELL, THE PRESSURE OF US BEING SUCKED OUT OF THE TEAR COULD CRUSH US. WE'LL MOST LIKELY SURVIVE THAT, BUT DEPENDING ON WHAT TYPE OF INJURY IT IS, WE COULD BE MAROONED ON THE SURFACE OR THROWN INTO SPACE.

WHAT?!

RELAX GUYS! YOUR BODY CAN PLUG UP A CUT BY FORMING A *BLOOD CLOT!*

RELAX, SAYS THE GIRL WHO CAN *FLY!*

WHEN THE PLATELETS REALISE THAT YOU'RE BLEEDING THEY COME RUNNING!

PLATELETS ARE THE FIRST STEP IN MAKING A CLOT!

PLATELETS ➪

WE'VE GOT A BREACH IN SECTOR 7. PLATELET TEAM ENGAGING!

THEY JOIN TOGETHER TO BLOCK THE HOLE!

WE'RE GOING TO NEED REINFORCEMENTS. STAT!

JUST DOING OUR JOB, MA'AM.

OH, THANK YOU! THANK YOU SO MUCH!

9

INSIDE THE KNEE JOINT.

WELCOME TO THE KNEE JOINT!

JOINTS ARE WHERE TWO BONES MEET.

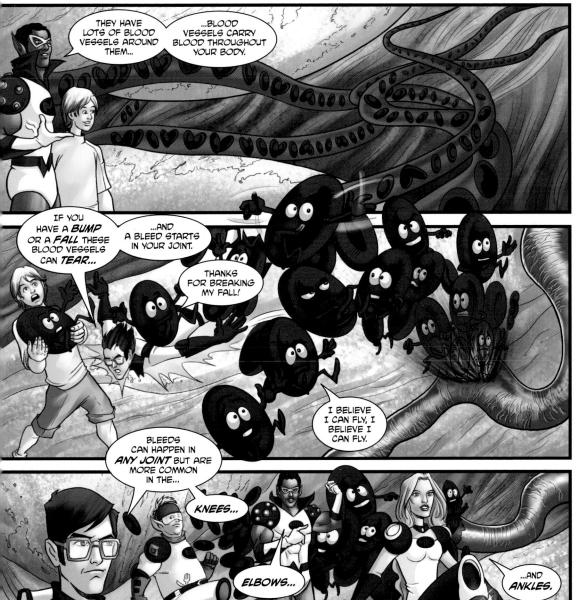

THEY HAVE LOTS OF BLOOD VESSELS AROUND THEM...

...BLOOD VESSELS CARRY BLOOD THROUGHOUT YOUR BODY.

IF YOU HAVE A *BUMP* OR A *FALL* THESE BLOOD VESSELS CAN *TEAR*...

...AND A BLEED STARTS IN YOUR JOINT.

THANKS FOR BREAKING MY FALL!

I BELIEVE I CAN FLY, I BELIEVE I CAN FLY.

BLEEDS CAN HAPPEN IN *ANY JOINT* BUT ARE MORE COMMON IN THE...

KNEES...

ELBOWS...

...AND *ANKLES.*

SOME KIDS BLEED IN *ONE JOINT* MORE THAN ANY OTHERS.

THIS IS CALLED A *TARGET JOINT.*

15

AHHHH! HOW DO WE STOP IT?

YOU'RE ALWAYS GOING TO HAVE HAEMOPHILIA, BUT YOU CAN TREAT IT.

TREATMENT DEPENDS ON WHAT *TYPE YOU HAVE.*

TO FIND OUT THE TYPE, YOUR DOCTOR OR NURSE WILL GIVE YOU A *BLOOD TEST.*

MAN, I HATE TESTS.

OKAY GASTRO, I EXAMINED YOUR BLOOD.

APPARENTLY YOUR BLOOD *IS* SPAGHETTI SAUCE.

HAEMOPHILIA B

HAEMOPHILIA A

OTHER ONES

THERE ARE 2 MAIN TYPES OF HAEMOPHILIA, AS WELL AS A FEW OTHER LESS COMMON ONES.

LET'S TAKE A LOOK.

18

ONCE THE DOCTOR KNOWS THE TYPE YOU HAVE, THERE ARE TWO WAYS TO TREAT IT... *R.I.C.E* AND *MEDICINES.*

I LOVE RICE.

YOU GOT ANYMORE OF THAT?

NOT THAT KIND OF RICE, GASTRO. R.I.C.E STANDS FOR *REST...*

I COULD USE A NAP.

ICE.

I BET YOU THINK YOU'RE PRETTY COOL, HUH?

COMPRESS.

AND *ELEVATE...* HIIIIYAAAAAH!

IF YOUR BLEED IS BAD, YOU'LL NEED TO TAKE MEDICINES TOO.

ONCE THE DOCTOR KNOWS WHAT TYPE YOU HAVE, YOU'LL GET *REPLACEMENT CLOTTING FACTORS.*

THEY ARE SO SIMILAR TO NATURAL CLOTTING FACTORS THAT YOUR BODY USUALLY CAN'T EVEN TELL THE DIFFERENCE.

REPLACEMENT CLOTTING FACTORS ARE MADE IN A LAB.

YOU LOOK LIKE ONE OF US...

ONLY BETTER LOOKING!

IT'S NOT VERY COMMON, BUT SOMETIMES YOU WILL HAVE TO HAVE A DIFFERENT TYPE OF MEDICINE IF REPLACEMENT CLOTTING FACTORS DON'T WORK.

WHY WOULD THEY NOT WORK?

YEAH, WHY WOULDN'T I WORK? I GOT THIS JOB IN THE BAG!

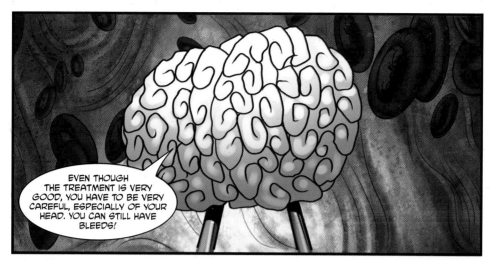

EVEN THOUGH THE TREATMENT IS VERY GOOD, YOU HAVE TO BE VERY CAREFUL, ESPECIALLY OF YOUR HEAD. YOU CAN STILL HAVE BLEEDS!

WITHOUT TREATMENT, YOU MIGHT GET *SPONTANEOUS* BLEEDING.

THIS MEANS YOU START BLEEDING EVEN IF YOU HAVEN'T HURT YOURSELF! BUT GOOD TREATMENT MAKES IT PRETTY RARE.

OR YOU MIGHT BE PLAYING OR RUNNING AROUND AND *NOT EVEN REMEMBER* KNOCKING YOURSELF, BUT YOU CAN STILL GET A BIG BRUISE AND BLOOD INTO YOUR JOINTS.

RIBS! GIMME, GIMME, GIMME!

BANG!!

TINGLING...

WARMTH...

PAIN...

...OR STIFFNESS.

THAT'S WHY IT'S IMPORTANT TO KNOW WHEN A BLEED STARTS.

YOU CAN TELL BY THE SIGNS.

IF YOU BLEED INTO YOUR JOINTS YOU MAY NOTICE SWELLING...

REMEMBER, YOU NEED TO STOP THE BLEED IMMEDIATELY IF YOU NOTICE ANY OF THESE SIGNS...

...EVEN IF YOU'RE IN THE MIDDLE OF SOMETHING OR WITH YOUR FRIENDS.

COME ON, GUYS, I WAS JUST GETTING TO KNOW MY CHICKEN CHOW MEIN!

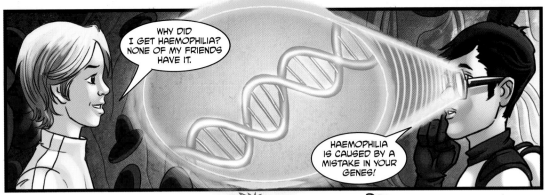

WHY DID I GET HAEMOPHILIA? NONE OF MY FRIENDS HAVE IT.

HAEMOPHILIA IS CAUSED BY A MISTAKE IN YOUR GENES!

GENES ARE THE *INSTRUCTIONS* THAT TELL YOUR BODY HOW TO WORK.

YOU GET ONE SET FROM YOUR MUM AND ONE SET FROM YOUR DAD!

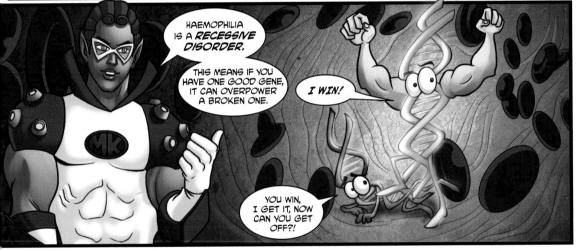

HAEMOPHILIA IS A *RECESSIVE DISORDER.*

THIS MEANS IF YOU HAVE ONE GOOD GENE, IT CAN OVERPOWER A BROKEN ONE.

I WIN!

YOU WIN, I GET IT, NOW CAN YOU GET OFF?!

GIRLS HAVE *TWO COPIES* OF THE GENE.

THIS MEANS THAT GIRLS USUALLY HAVE ONE WORKING COPY AND SO CAN'T GET HAEMOPHILIA A OR B.

NICE T-SHIRT, SKIN!

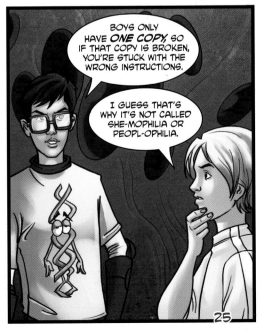

BOYS ONLY HAVE *ONE COPY*, SO IF THAT COPY IS BROKEN, YOU'RE STUCK WITH THE WRONG INSTRUCTIONS.

I GUESS THAT'S WHY IT'S NOT CALLED SHE-MOPHILIA OR PEOPL-OPHILIA.

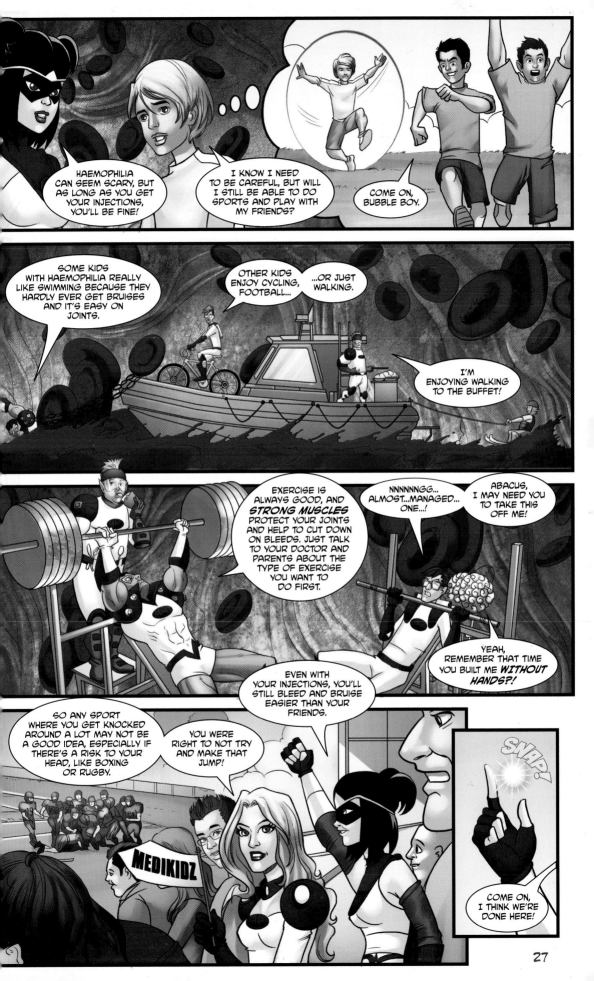

BACK ON EARTH...

WHOA, I'VE GOT TO FIND PAT AND GAVIN AND TELL THEM WHAT HAPPENED!

GUYS! YOU WILL NOT BELIEVE WHAT HAPPENED!

YOU FLEW HERE ON YOUR CHICKEN WINGS?

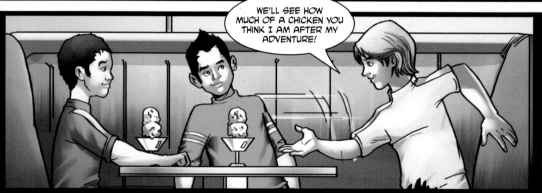

WE'LL SEE HOW MUCH OF A CHICKEN YOU THINK I AM AFTER MY ADVENTURE!

I GOT ZAPPED TO A PLANET CALLED MEDILAND!

...SO THE CUT WAS LIKE A BLACK HOLE SUCKING US OUT...

SO THE *FIBRINATOR* SHOOTS THIS FIBRIN MESH WHICH HELPS CLOT...

BUT MY IMMUNE SYSTEM ARMY SOMETIMES ATTACKS THE NEW OPERATOR!

...MEANING IT'S A GENETIC DISORDER, BUT AS LONG AS I TAKE MY MEDICINE AND AM CAREFUL, I CAN LIVE A TOTALLY NORMAL LIFE!

MAN, I HAD NO IDEA ABOUT YOUR HAEMOPHILIA!

YEAH, I TAKE IT ALL BACK.

IF I WERE YOU I'D BE LIVING IN A BUBBLE!

I THOUGHT ABOUT THAT, BUT THEN I WOULDN'T BE VERY *BRAVE!*